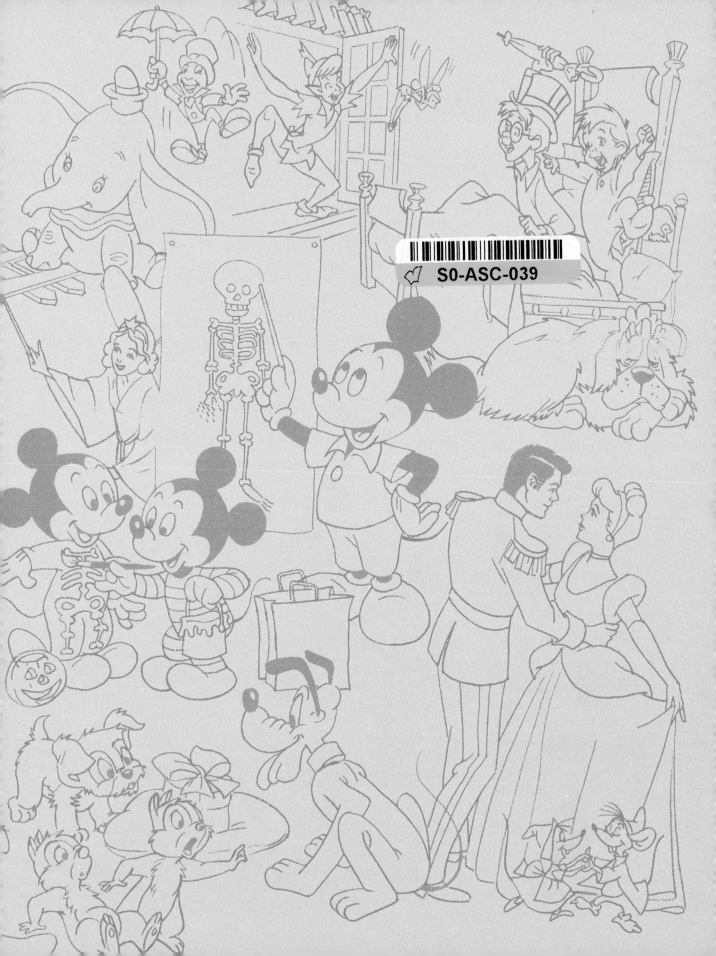

This book belongs to

_____

WALT DISNEY® VOLUME 12
IT'S A SMALL WORLD

WALT DISNEY FUN-TO-LEARN LIBRARY

ISBN 1-885222-03-3
Advance Publishers Inc., P.O. Box 2607, Winter Park, FL. 32790
Printed in the United States of America
0987654321

Have you ever wondered what children in other countries do for fun? If your answer is yes, you are in for a treat.

Today is It's-a-Small-World Day at Morty and Ferdie's school, and *you* are invited. Everyone is very excited. The children are going to taste foods from other lands and learn lively folk dances. They'll even get to try on some costumes.

Best of all, Mickey is here! Mickey has been around the world many times and has visited children from every land. He is going to tell us all about the countries he has visited, and show us some of his pictures.

Just turn the page and you, too, can share in the fun of It's-a-Small-World Day.

Yvette and her friend Mark live in Canada. They love to go ice fishing in the long, cold winter.

Each year, they help Yvette's parents drag a little wooden cabin out onto the frozen river. A fire helps to keep the cabin warm inside. Then the two friends simply make a hole in the ice through an opening in the cabin floor. They bait their hooks, and wait for the fish to bite.

"Come inside," calls Yvette. "It's much more fun in here."

It's a very, very merry Christmas in Mexico. Carlos and Alicia are going to break a piñata with their friends. A piñata is a big hollow toy filled with candy and little toys and fruit all wrapped up together in bright-colored paper.

The guests take turns trying to break open the piñata with a stick until—SMACK, out fall the goodies.

Astrud and Roberto live in Rio de Janeiro. At carnival time, there is no place they would rather be. For one week at Eastertime, schools and shops close so that everyone can go to parties and dances. The streets are decorated with flowers, and special bands come to the city to play Brazilian tunes called Sambas.

What are Rosita and Paco doing with all those paper bags
full of balloons? They are getting ready for carnival time in Peru.
They have brought brightly colored powders to mix with water.
Then they will fill each balloon with a different-colored water.

Rosita and Paco join in the biggest water fight ever.
Even mothers and fathers enjoy the fun. It looks
as though the children have found the best
place to shower their friends with color.
Splash! Goofy is blushing red all over!
Soon everyone in the town will look like
a gaily colored Easter egg.

In winter, Norway is a land of beautiful snowy mountains. Almost everyone in Norway knows how to ski. Kirsten learned to ski when she was only three years old. Other children might slide down the mountain the way Anders does, on a round piece of metal that looks like a pie tin.

Can you imagine waking in the middle of the night to see the sun shining? In Norway, the summer sun shines almost as brightly at midnight as it does at midday! That is why Norway is called "the Land of the Midnight Sun."

Anders and Kirsten stay up all night to celebrate the first day of summer. The children stack all the wood and paper they can find in great big piles. Then, at the stroke of midnight, their parents set the piles on fire. Everyone cheers. Summer is here!

Tommy and Jill live in London, England's capital city. If you like stories about queens and princesses, palaces and coaches, or horses and guards, in London you'll find they come true! Today, Tommy and Jill have joined Mickey and his friends outside Buckingham Palace, the home of the queen. A grand procession is just starting out through the palace gates.

You can always tell the palace guards by their splendid uniforms and their serious expressions. Wouldn't you like to try on one of those tall, furry hats?

Paris is the capital city of France and one
of the prettiest cities in the world. Perhaps this is why
so many artists have chosen to live there. Mickey is having
his picture painted by one of them now. It looks as though Goofy
could use a few lessons.

Gilbert and Marie have just been to the bakery to buy breakfast. Do
you know what they are carrying under their arms? Those special long
loaves are called *baguettes*. The children are going to share their fresh-
baked bread with Mickey and Goofy. Don't you wish that you could
join them?

Kindergarten is a German word meaning "garden of children." For Hans and Greta, the first day of school is a happy one. Each of them gets a giant cone filled with candy to sweeten their day. How handsome they look, wearing their brand-new school clothes.

"Smile, please," says Donald. Poor Huey thought he was getting a new hat!

Jan and Gretchen live in the Netherlands. Today is Gretchen's birthday, and she is having a party.

There is so much water in the Netherlands that some of Gretchen's guests arrive by boat. Mickey and his nephews are wearing special wooden shoes called *klompschoen* to help keep their feet dry. "Hurry up, the party's beginning," calls Jan, as they click-clack up to the house.

Instead of fairy tales, Greek children love to hear stories about their favorite gods, goddesses, and ancient heroes. The make-believe gods could make thunder when they were angry, and rainbows when they were glad. Morty and Ferdie think that Goofy would make a great Greek hero, but Mickey is not so sure.

Nick and Ana each have a donkey to take them up the narrow mountain trails around their village. Huey and Dewey are having fun— but whatever happened to Donald?

The Festival of the Crickets is a great favorite of Maria and Dominic of Italy. To celebrate spring, the children buy a cricket and a miniature cage for it. Maria and Dominic take good care of their new little friend. They feed it bits of lettuce and listen to it sing.

At the end of the day, they set it free.

Abram and Ruth of Israel live on a kibbutz. This is a big farm where
many mothers and fathers and their children all live together. Each
person helps with the job he or she does best. And with so many people
at the table, dinnertime is always fun.

Afterwards, everyone helps to do the dishes.

Today, all the schoolchildren will dress up in costumes. They will go
to a carnival where they will sing and dance. This is how Jewish children
celebrate Purim, the feast of the great Queen Esther.

Have you ever slept in a tent beneath the stars? Fatima and Omar of Egypt sleep in one every night. Because the desert is so dry, they take their tent, goats, and camels with them from place to place in search of water.

Look where they are sleeping tonight. Those huge buildings are the Great Pyramids, the tombs where three famous kings, or pharaohs, of Egypt were buried—long, long ago. And there, crouching in the sand, is the mighty Sphinx. This huge statue, with the head of a human and the body of a lion, is guarding the Pyramids from all who would harm them.

For Togbi and Kofi of Ghana, today is a very special day. The whole village will celebrate because the people are getting a new chief. Here comes the parade now!

Togbi and Kofi's father, the new chief, is being carried in a grand procession through the village. The colorful umbrellas whirl and twirl to the rhythm of the talking drums. How proud the children must feel.

No, Goofy, it isn't raining. The umbrellas shade the chief from the blazing-hot sun.

Ilunga of Zaire can't wait to become 13 years old. For only then will he be old enough to wear one of the wonderful masks of his tribe. There are ugly masks to frighten away evil spirits, and happy ones to wear at celebrations. Some masks are the faces of animals. Which one would you choose?

Krishna and Chandra of India have left their tiny village to explore the city for a day.

There's so much for them to see! The women look lovely as they walk down the street in graceful saris. By the curb, camels share parking spaces with cars. And on a corner, Krishna and Chandra notice some pretty things to buy. How grown-up they feel, as they choose presents to take home for their mother.

When Krishna and Chandra return to their village, still more excitement awaits them. A special autumn festival will brighten the village. There will be puppet shows and parades. Everyone will wear their finest clothes. Even the elephants will have their toenails polished and wear colorful designs painted on their trunks and sides.

In Moscow, the capital city of the Soviet Union, there is a special school for children who want to become circus performers. Here, Natasha learns the trapeze, wire walking, and acrobatics, as well as reading and arithmetic.

If she becomes a bear trainer, she will travel all over the world with Boris the bear and the famous Moscow Circus. Take a bow, Natasha. Perhaps some day, you will be the star of the show.

Mischa thinks Leningrad is the most beautiful city in the Soviet Union. He loves to show off its palaces, statues, and fountains. His favorite place is the children's park at Peterhof. It's a wonderland, with magic fountains that spring up right beneath your feet when you least expect them.

Mei Chu and Kwang Ling live in the People's Republic of China, the country with the largest number of people in the world.

Imagine the excitement as so many people celebrate holidays together. For Mei Chu and Kwang Ling, the New Year is the happiest time of all, because the holiday lasts for several days.

This is the evening of the Lantern Festival. On this last day of the New Year celebrations, huge lions parade through the streets. The children wave paper flowers and scatter confetti. Red envelopes with money are hung in doorways for good luck. And all around, firecrackers hiss and explode in the air.

In Japan, little girls love dolls so much that they have a special Doll's Day every year to honor them. Today, Yasuko has some new dolls to add to her collection. Of course, the emperor and empress dolls will go on the top shelf because they are the fanciest.

Yasuko's friends arrive for her party looking like beautiful butterflies in their favorite kimonos. She serves them delicious rice cakes she has prepared herself.

Then they will visit the homes of other friends, to admire their dolls, and to eat their special food.

On Boy's Day in Japan, you can
see fish swimming in the sky! They're not real
fish, of course, but beautifully colored kites that
are shaped like fish.

Yoji has worked for days to make a perfect
kite. It is hollow, so the wind will fill it up. And
he has used such bright-colored paper that all his
friends will see his kite in the Boy's Day parade.

Elena and Louis of the Philippines have a very special home—they live in a bamboo house built high over the water. When they want to take a bath, all they have to do is jump out their front door. Splash! That's Huey jumping in now!

Children in the Philippines have found another way to use bamboo in a special dance called the *tinikling*. Goofy, Elena, and Louis dance in and out of long bamboo poles, clapped together to a rhythmical beat. It's fun, but watch out for your toes, Goofy!

Bob and Diane live in the "outback" region of Australia. There are no schools there because children live so far from one another. That's why Bob and Diane learn their lessons from a radio program called "The School of the Air."

And if Diane or Bob become sick, their parents will telephone for the flying doctor, who will arrive within minutes in an airplane.

After lessons are over,
it's time for fun.

Did you ever hear of a bird called a kookaburra? Or have you ever heard of a wallaby? That's a little kangaroo. These are just two of the strange and wonderful animals Bob and Diane might see as they wander out their front door.

When you throw a stick, you may ask your dog to bring it back to you. But Australian children throw special curved sticks called boomerangs that circle back when they are thrown. Watch out for that boomerang, Donald, you'd better duck!

Steve and his friend Christy live in New York City, the city with the most people in the United States of America. Whenever the children have visitors, they like to take them to the Statue of Liberty. This huge statue holds her torch high to welcome all who visit her. From the top of her crown, you will have a wonderful view of one of the most famous skylines in the world—that of New York City.

Did you ever pretend you were a cowboy or a cowgirl? That's what Bob and Susanna want to be when they grow up. They live on a cattle ranch in Oklahoma, so they get plenty of practice riding and roping. They'll show off what they can do at the rodeo today. Here comes Goofy on a bucking bronco—how long do you think he can stay on?

The children at Morty and Ferdie's school agree that there's one thing children all over the world like to do—they like to have fun. What about you?

All of the children want to thank Mickey for helping them celebrate their special day.

תּוֹדָה.
gracias
takk
ありがとう。
merci

In Japan, children say *arigato* for
    "thank you."
Mexican children say *gracias*.
Norwegian children say *takk*.
In Israel, children say *toda*.
French children say *merci*.
    And to all the children Mickey
says, "Thank *you*, everyone,
thank *you*."